CONDUCTOR

Wedding Essentials

CONTENTS

This book is arranged for 2 B-flat trumpets, French horn, trombone, and tuba. The music in this book is from the personal library of Canadian Brass and has been performed and recorded by Canadian Brass.

To access companion recorded performances online, visit:
www.halleonard.com/mylibrary

Enter Code
5620-4836-1422-0187

7777 W. BLUEMOUND RD. P.O. BOX 13819 MILWAUKEE, WI 53213

www.canadianbrass.com
www.halleonard.com

"AIR"
from *Water Music*

Handel
(1685-1759)
Trans. By Walter Barnes

22 'Air' from Water Music *continued*

29

LARGO

From *Xerxes*

George Frideric Handel
(1685-1759)
arranged by Walter Barnes

PRAYER

From *Hansel and Gretel*

Engelbert Humperdinck
(1854-1921)
arranged by Henry Charles Smith

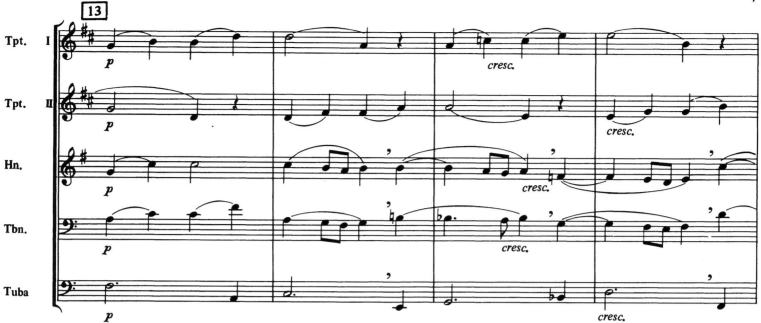

AIR ON THE G STRING
from Suite No. 3

J. S. Bach
(1685–1750)
Trans. by A. Frackenpohl

For shorter version, play 1st section (m. 1-5 and 2nd ending) once without piccolo trumpet.
Then 2nd section (m. 8-19) once with piccolo doubling trumpet in octaves.

CANON

Johann Pachelbel
(1653-1706)
arranged by Walter Barnes

FANFARE
from ORFEO

Claudio Monteverdi
(1567-1643)
adapted and arranged by Stephen McNeff

Da Capo al Fine

TRUMPET TUNE AND AYRE

Henry Purcell
(1659-1695)
arranged by Walter Barnes

18

TRUMPET VOLUNTARY

Stanley
(1713-1786)
arranged by Walter Barnes

2003, 1986, Canadian Brass Publications LTD
International Copyright Secured

34 Trumpet Voluntary *continued*

TRUMPET VOLUNTARY

Jeremiah Clarke
(1673-1707)
arranged by Walter Barnes

Allargando

BRIDAL CHORUS
from LOHENGRIN

Richard Wagner
(1813-1883)
edited by Canadian Brass

WEDDING MARCH

Felix Mendelssohn
(1809–1847)
Adapted by Ryan Anthony

RONDEAU
(Theme from *Masterpiece Theatre*)

Jean-Joseph Mouret
(1682-1738)
arranged by Walter Barnes

OTHER APPROPRIATE WEDDING PIECES

Prelude
Fantasie (Bach)
Sheep May Safely Graze (Bach)*
Where e'er you walk (Handel)*

Prelude or Solo
Bist du bei mir (Bach, attr.)

Prelude or Processional
Jesu, Joy of Man's Desiring from *Cantata 147* (Bach)
Wachet auf (Sleepers Awake) from *Cantata 140* (Bach)*

Processional or Recessional
Trumpet Voluntary (Boyce)
Prelude from *Te Deum* (Charpentier)
March (Allegro spiritoso) from *Heroic Suite* (Telemann)

Solo
Ave Maria (Bach/Gounod)
Ave Maria (Schubert)

Recessional
Ode to Joy (Beethoven)
Allegro from *Water Music* (Handel)*
Arrival of the Queen of Sheba from *Solomon* (Handel)*
La Rejouissance (The Rejoicing) from *Music for the Royal Fireworks* (Handel)

More Recommended Music for Weddings
My heart ever faithful from *Cantata 68* (Bach)
Pavane (Fauré)
Pie Jesu from *Requiem, Op. 48* (Fauré)
Panis Angelicus (Franck)
Let the Bright Seraphim from *Samson* (Handel)*
Psalm XIX: The Heavens Declare (Marcello)
Toccata (Martini)
Alleluia from *Exsultate, jubilate* (Mozart)*
Ave verum corpus (Mozart)*
Agnus Dei (Palestrina)
Sonata for Two Trumpets and Brass (Purcell)*
Concerto in C (Vivaldi)*

*Canadian Brass publications

Additional Sacred Publications from Canadian Brass
Distributed by Hal Leonard Corp.

Hymns for Brass (Easy Level)
- 50488754 Trumpet 1
- 50488755 Trumpet 2
- 50488756 Horn
- 50488757 Trombone
- 50488758 Tuba
- 50488759 Conductor

Single Quintet Titles
- 50488730 All Breathing Life (Bach/H.C. Smith)
- 50488791 Amazing Grace (Henderson)
- 50483602 Ave Verum Corpus (Mozart/Watkin)
- 50488751 Hallelujah Chorus (Handel/Mills)
- 50507180 Hallelujah Chorus (with Organ)
- 50483726 Hanukah Trilogy (Ohanian/Romm)
- 50396690 Just a Closer Walk (Gillis)
- 50482281 Nearer, My God, to Thee (Henderson)
- 50396130 O Come, All Ye Faithful & Joy to the World (with Organ) (Gillis)
- 50489342 O Come, Emmanuel & I Wonder as I Wander (w/Organ) (Gillis)
- 50489343 O Holy Night (with Organ) (Adam/Frackenpohl)
- 50396170 Sheep May Safely Graze (Bach/Watts)

Double Quintet Titles
- 50396740 Jesu, Joy of Man's Desiring (Bach/Mills)
- 50396900 Magnificat (Pachelbel/Frackenpohl)